CLASSIC WISDOM COLLECTION

TODAY'S QUESTIONS. TIMELESS ANSWERS.

Looking for time-tested guidance for the dilemmas of the spiritual life? Find it in the company of the wise spiritual masters of our Catholic tradition.

Courage in Chaos

CLASSIC WISDOM COLLECTION

Courage in Chaos

Wisdom from Francis de Sales

Compiled by Kathryn Hermes, FSP
Foreword by Paulamarie Splaine, FSP

Pauline
BOOKS & MEDIA
Boston

Library of Congress Cataloging-in-Publication Data

Francis, de Sales, Saint, 1567-1622.
  [Selections. English. 2012]
  Courage in chaos : wisdom from Francis de Sales / compiled by
Kathryn Hermes ; foreword by Paulamarie Splaine.
      p. cm. -- (Catholic wisdom collection)
  Summary: "Saint Francis de Sales offers practical advice on how to
trust God in the midst of chaos"--Provided by publisher.
  Includes bibliographical references (p. 89).
  ISBN 0-8198-1597-7 (pbk.)
  1. Spiritual life--Catholic Church. I. Hermes, Kathryn. II. Title.
  BX2350.3.F72 2012
  248.4'82--dc23

                          2011027852

Scripture quotations are transcribed from the original translations of
Francis de Sales's works.

Cover design by Rosana Usselmann

Cover photo by Mary Emmanuel Alves, FSP

Published by Pauline Books & Media, 50 Saint Pauls Avenue, Boston,
MA 02130-3491

Printed in the U.S.A.

www.pauline.org

Pauline Books & Media is the publishing house of the Daughters of
Saint Paul, an international congregation of women religious serving
the Church with the communications media.

1 2 3 4 5 6 7 8 9   16 15 14 13 12

For all those who seek.

And for all those who try to show the way.

Contents

Foreword

Even those who are too young to remember the rebelliousness of the 1960s today experience the profound insecurity which has cloaked the world since 9/11. (Not to mention the subsequent wars or recent devastating natural disasters.) My relationship with the gentle Francis de Sales began in the 1960s, and ever since he has been both my comfort and my guide.

I was a child of those years of social upheaval marked by the Vietnam War, riots on college campuses, the "hippie" culture, and the general rejection of the established moral laws. All of this added to the confusion of my own teenage years.

One teacher, noting my cynical attitude, gave me a bit of advice: "It is easier to catch flies with a teaspoon of honey than with a barrel full of vinegar." Saint Francis de Sales was the wise person who not only wrote these words but lived them in the midst of the chaos of his own time. I was curious from that first mention of his name; what else might he have to say to me?

Shortly after that I entered the convent, and Saint Francis de Sales sought me out. I found the book *Saint Francis de Sales and His Friends* in the library, and I eagerly read about this intriguing saint who would point my life in a new direction.

I reached out to him as to an experienced and kind advisor for my heart, for even in the convent the forces of change were whirling. Francis and his writings were balm to my spirit during a time that tried us all.

Francis de Sales was born August 21, 1567, into a family of French nobility from the region of Savoy. His parents provided him with an excellent education in the classics at the University of Paris and sent him on for a doctorate in law in Padua, Italy. Francis's father dreamed of seeing his son in the Senate of Savoy one day, but Francis had other ideas.

Soon after his studies were completed, Francis was appointed "provost,"[1] or judicial vicar of the bishop, in his native Geneva-Annecy diocese. This appointment forced him to break the news to his father that he wanted to become a priest. Meanwhile the bishop was already sending off speedy letters to Rome asking permission for a quick ordination for this man who had been so well prepared for such a step.

After his ordination, Canon Francis de Sales was not content to sit in an office. He set out into the countryside, visiting the people, seeking to make friends and let them know he was available to help in any way he could.

Although Francis was young, intelligent, well prepared, and very enthusiastic, he still needed to learn to be tactful, a trait that soon became the hallmark of his life, writings, and relationships.

Bishop de Granier of Geneva received a request to send missionaries to Le Chablais, a section of Savoy situated between Annecy and Switzerland. Sixty years earlier Le Chablais had been taken over by militant Protestants who had imposed the Reformed Faith. Many Catholic churches were destroyed, priests were expelled from the territory, religious were disbanded, and all forms of Catholic worship and practice were forbidden. Francis de Sales's offer to take up this difficult work of reinvigorating Catholicism in the region was immediately accepted. Although the diocese had no funds to give Canon Francis and his cousin Canon Louis, who accompanied him on this dangerous mission, the two set out on September 14, 1594 to minister to the 60,000 people of Le Chablais, 100 of whom were faithful Catholics. Months of hardship prompted Canon Louis to return home, fearful that he would be unable to bear the rigors of the coming winter. Francis continued on alone, and after seven months a lawyer named Poncet asked to be re-admitted to the Church. This was the beginning of the Church's rebirth: a costly victory that had been slow in coming.

Despite great danger and several attempts on his life, Francis copied excerpts of his sermons and slipped them under doors. In time someone had them printed and made available as posters for display in public places. These tracts, which were more like scholarly essays, examined the problems that separated Calvinists and Catholics, and slowly bore fruit. Baron D'Avully joined Poncet in returning to the Catholic Faith in the spring of 1595. The conversions of such leading figures led to thousands of Calvinists reconciling with the Catholic Church. By his preaching, his writing, and his affectionate personality, Francis prompted many to rethink their decision to leave the Church and embrace Protestantism. By 1598, through his untiring efforts, the majority of the people of the district had returned to the Catholic faith.

When Bishop de Granier died, Francis was appointed Bishop of Geneva-Annecy, at age thirty-five. He brought to this new responsibility a wondrous array of talents, intellect, and virtue acquired in his many previous roles.

Francis de Sales continues to be revered for his many writings, in particular for "An Introduction to the Devout Life" and "Treatise on the Love of God."[2] In his 20,000 letters he has left pearls of faith and wisdom, the stuff of the saints; and together with Saint Jane Frances de Chantal in the foundation of the Institute of the Visitation of the Blessed Virgin (Visitation Sisters), he blessed the Church with a community of holiness.

While in Lyons, France, with the nobles of Savoy, Francis suffered a stroke and died on December 28, 1622. He was beatified in 1661 and canonized four years later. Pope Pius IX declared him a doctor of the Church in 1877. His feast day is celebrated on January 29.

What made Francis a great bishop? It seems to me it was his spirit of hope and interior freedom and his confidence in God's love that were the foundations of his activity. In his life, this core of fidelity and righteousness that he had so patiently and firmly refined was the source of his unflappable kindness, his careful and sure direction, and his courageous administration of a diocese so in need of renewal and reform. It was also no surprise that so many turned to Bishop Francis above all for spiritual advice and for help in facing the hundreds of daily problems that require the calm trust that is born of a deep and convinced faith. Saint Francis de Sales, with respect, precision, wisdom, and some great wit, listened to all who asked his guidance.

Saint Francis struggled in his own life and in his responsibilities as bishop with how to be a Christian in an insecure world. The same problems that plagued him and his people, trouble us today:

— How can I be rich in spirit when I am struggling with poverty?

— How can I be poor in spirit when I have all I need and more of this world's goods?

— Can I really learn to live my life without anxiety?

— How can I balance helping others with caring for my own loved ones?

— Can I ever fit a decent moment for prayer into my day?

— Gentleness—where can I find the strength of spirit for this?

— How can I master my anger?

— Is it possible to live the Gospel in a litigious society? Or will I just be taken advantage of?

— I am exhausted by the number of roles I have to fulfill and things I'm expected to do. How do I find peace of heart?

Francis de Sales has been, for me, a friend who has withstood the test of time. He has faced down the frightening tempests in this writer's heart, having dealt with them first in his own. His faith in the providence of God and his strong and tender love for others call out to me to discover how peaceful I can be when my heart is safe and strong with the Lord. I have seen, as Francis did, that, if I am willing to cooperate with the ways of Divine Providence in my daily life, being there for those who need me is not a roadblock or a distraction but a *way*—a way of following and mirroring the Gospel message, even without words.

In Saint Francis de Sales's words, so wise and urbane, may you catch a glimmer of the fire of faith and the breadth of love that kept him cheerful and steadfast to the end—a firm, loving, shining mirror of Christ, whom he served so well. With our hands clasped in God's, like Francis, we will never walk alone.

I

A Gentle Way

To live in a gentle way, it is important to respect our-selves, never growing irritated with ourselves or our imperfections. Although it is but reasonable that we should be displeased and grieved at our own faults, we need to guard against being bitter, angry, or fretful about them. Many people fall into the error of being angry because they have been angry, or impatient because they have given way to impatience; this keeps them in a chronic state of irritation, strengthens the impressions made, and prepares one for a fresh fall on the first occasion. Moreover, all this anger and irritation against one's self fosters pride, springing as it does from self-love, which is disturbed and upset by its own imperfection.

What we need is a quiet, steady, firm displeasure at our own faults. A judge who speaks deliberately and calmly when he gives sentence will punish vice more effectively than speaking in an impetuous and passionate way, for in that case he would be punishing not so much the actual crimes before him, as his own perceptions of them. We can chasten ourselves far better by a quiet and steadfast repentance than by eager hasty efforts at penitence, prompted not so much by the weight of our faults, as by our own negative feelings and inclinations.

Believe me, as a parent's tender, affectionate admonishment carries far more weight with his child than does anger and sternness, so, when we judge our own heart to be guilty, if we treat it gently, rather in a spirit of pity than anger, encouraging it to make amends, our repentance will be much deeper and more lasting than it would be if it were stirred up by vehemence and wrath. Suppose that I am trying to conquer my vanity, and yet I have fallen into that sin. Instead of taking myself to task as abominable and wretched for breaking so many resolutions, calling myself unfit to lift up my eyes to heaven, disloyal, faithless, and the like, I need to deal with myself quietly and with compassion: "My heart! So soon fallen again into the snare! Well now, rise up again bravely and fall no more. Seek

God's mercy, hope in him, ask him to keep you from falling again, and begin to walk on the pathway of humility once more. You must be more careful from now on." This will be the surest way to carry out a steadfast and substantial effort against this special fault. We can add any suitable external means, and this includes the advice of our director. If any one does not find this gentle dealing sufficient for himself, he could use sterner self-rebuke and admonition, provided only that whatever indignation he may rouse against himself, he can bring it all in the end to a tender, loving trust in God, treading in the footsteps of that great penitent who cried out to his troubled soul: "Why are you downcast, my soul; why do you groan within me? Wait for God, whom I shall praise again, my savior and my God" (Ps 42:6).

So then, when you have fallen, lift up your heart quietly, humbling yourself deeply before God for your frailty, without marveling that you fell, since there is no cause to marvel because weakness is weak, infirmity, infirm, and frailty, frail. Sincerely regret that you should have offended God, and begin anew to seek the grace you need, with a very deep trust in God's mercy, and with a bold, brave heart.

— Excerpt from *Introduction to the Devout Life,* Part 3: Chapter 9

II

Be Just and Fair

Reason is the special characteristic of humans, and yet it is a rare thing to find really reasonable people, since self-love often hinders right reason, and beguiles us without our realizing it into all manner of trifling, yet dangerous acts of injustice and untruth, which, like the little foxes in the Song of Songs, "damage our vines" (Sg 2:15). Precisely because they are trifling, people pay no attention to them, and, being numerous, they do untold harm. Let me give you some examples of what I mean.

We find fault with our neighbor very readily for small matters, while we pass over great things in ourselves. We strive to sell at an inflated price and buy with discounts.

We are eager to deal out strict justice to others, but just as eager to obtain indulgence for ourselves. We expect a good interpretation to be put on all we say, but we are sensitive and critical of our neighbor's words. We expect him to let us buy whatever we want of his, for we have the money, when it would be more reasonable to let him keep his possession, if he desires to do so, and for us to keep our gold. We are vexed with him because he will not accommodate us, while perhaps he has better reason to be vexed with us for wanting to disturb him. If we have a liking for any one particular thing, we despise all else, and reject whatever does not precisely suit our taste. If someone who works for us is unacceptable to us, or we have once caught him in error, he is sure to be wrong in our eyes whatever he may do, and we often block his efforts, and look haughtily on him, while, on the other hand, someone who happens to please us is always sure to be right. Sometimes even parents show unfair preference for a child endowed with personal gifts over one who has some physical imperfection. We put the rich before the poor, although the rich may be less worthy of our honor, and we even give preference to well-dressed people. We are strict in protecting our own rights, but we expect others to yield their own for our interests. We complain freely of our neighbors, but we do not like them to make any complaints about us. Whatever we do for them appears very great in our sight, but what they do for us counts as nothing. In a word, we have a very gentle, liberal, and courteous heart toward ourselves, and one which is hard, rigorous, and severe toward our neighbor. We have two scales, one weighted to measure our own goods to the best advantage, and the other to weigh our neighbors' to the worst. Even Holy Scripture tells us that "those who tell lies to one another speak with deceiving lips and a double heart" (Ps 12:3).

Be just and fair in all you do. Always put yourself in your neighbor's place, and put him into yours, and then you will judge fairly. Sell as you would buy, and buy as you would sell, and the buying and selling will both be honest. The acts of injustice I mentioned above seem small because they do not demand restitution, and we have, after all, only taken that which we can demand using the strict letter of the law; but, nevertheless, they greatly need to be corrected, since, while on the one hand they are mere cheating tricks, on the other, they offend against fairness and charity. No one ever loses by being generous, noble-hearted, and courteous. Be sure, then, to examine your dealings with your neighbor often, and see if your heart is just toward him, as you would have his heart just toward you, were things reversed—this is the true test of reason.

— Excerpt from *Introduction to the Devout Life,* Part 3: Chapter 36

III

Be Not Too Anxious

The care and diligence due in our ordinary affairs differs greatly from worry, anxiety, and restlessness. The angels care for our salvation and seek it diligently, but they are wholly free from anxiety and solicitude. Since care and diligence naturally accompany their love, anxiety would be wholly inconsistent with their happiness. Although care and diligence can go hand in hand with calmness and peace, these angelic properties cannot abide together with solicitude or anxiety, much less with overeagerness.

Therefore, be careful and diligent in all your affairs. God, who entrusts them to you, wants you to give them your best effort. But try not to be too anxious or solicitous, that is to say, do not set about your work with restlessness and excitement, and do not give way to bustle and eagerness in what you do. Any form of excitement affects both judgment and reason, and hinders a competent performance of the very task which is making us anxious.

Our Lord, rebuking Martha, said, "Martha, Martha, you are anxious and worried about many things" (Lk 10:41). If she had been simply diligent, she would not have been worried, but giving way to disquiet and anxiety, she grew hurried and troubled, and for that our Lord reproved her. The rivers which flow gently through our plains bear barges of rich merchandise, and the gracious rains which fall softly on the land fertilize it to bear the fruits of the earth. But if the rivers swell into torrents, they hinder commerce and devastate the country, and violent storms and tempests do the same. No work done with impetuosity and excitement was ever well done; hence the old proverb, "Make haste slowly," is a good one. The Son of Sirach said, "One may toil and struggle and drive, and fall short all the more" (Sir 11:11). We are always finished soon enough when we do our tasks well. The bumble bee makes far more noise and clamor than the honey bee, but it makes only wax, not honey. In the same manner, those who are restless and eager, or full of noisy solicitude, never do much, nor do they do it well.

Flies harass us more by their numbers than by their sting. Similarly, great matters disturb us less than a multitude of small affairs. Accept the duties which are entrusted to you quietly, and try to fulfill them methodically, one after another. If you attempt to do everything at once, or with confusion, you will only burden yourself with your own exertions, and by entangling your mind, you will probably be overwhelmed and accomplish nothing.

In all your affairs rely on God's Providence, through which alone your plans can succeed. Meanwhile, on your part, work on in quiet cooperation with God, and then rest satisfied that if you have entrusted your work entirely to God, you will always obtain that measure of success which is best for you, whether it seems so or not in your own judgment.

Imitate a little child, who holds tight with one hand to his father's, while with the other gathers blackberries from the wayside hedge. Even so, while you gather and use this world's goods with one hand, always let the other be secure in your Heavenly Father's hand, and look round from time to time to make sure that he is satisfied with what you are doing, at home or abroad. Beware of letting his hand go, seeking to make or receive more—if God forsakes you, you will fall to the ground at the very first step. When your ordinary work or business is not particularly engrossing, let your heart be fixed more on God than on it;

and if the work be such as to require your undivided attention, then pause from time to time and look to God, even as navigators do who set their course for the harbor by looking up at the heavens rather than down into the deeps on which they sail. Doing this, you will see that God will work with you, in you, and for you, and your work will be blessed.

— Excerpt from *Introduction to the Devout Life,* Part 3: Chapter 10

IV

True Discipleship

When God created the world, he commanded each tree to bear its own specific fruit (cf. Gn 1:12); and likewise he bids Christians, the living trees of his Church, to bring forth fruits of loyal discipleship, each one according to his circumstances and vocation. A different exercise of discipleship is required of all, and this discipleship must be adapted to the strength, the occupation, and the duties of each individual. I ask you, would it be fitting that a bishop should seek to lead the solitary life of a monk? What if the father of a family were as unconcerned in making material provision for the family's future as a vowed religious. Or if workers spent all day in church.

Would not such practices be exaggerated and impossible to carry out? Yet such a mistake is often made, and the world, which cannot or will not distinguish between real discipleship and the indiscretion of those who consider themselves devout, grumbles and finds fault with a disciple's life, which is in no way connected to these errors. True discipleship hinders no one; on the contrary, it perfects everything; and that which runs counter to the rightful vocation of any person is, you may be sure, a mistaken devotion. Aristotle says that the bee sucks honey from flowers without damaging them, leaving them as whole and fresh as it found them. True discipleship does better still, for it not only interferes with no vocation or duty, but it adorns and beautifies them all. Throw precious stones into honey, and each will grow more brilliant according to its color; in the same way, everyone fulfills their own special calling better when done in a spirit of discipleship—family duties are lighter, married love is deeper, service to our country more faithful, in short every kind of occupation becomes more acceptable and better performed where this loyal discipleship is the guide.

It is an error to seek to banish spirituality from the soldier's guardroom, the merchant's shop, the offices of government, or the family home. Of course, a purely contemplative devotion, such as is proper to the religious and monastic life, cannot be followed in these secular voca-tions, but there are various types of spirituality well suited to lead those whose calling is secular along the paths of perfection. The Old Testament gives us examples in Abraham, Isaac, Jacob, David, Job, Tobias, Sarah, Rebecca, and Judith. And in the New Testament, we read of Saint Joseph, Lydia, and Saint Crispin, who led perfectly devout lives while carrying out their trades. We have Saint Anne, Martha, Saint Monica, Aquila, and Priscilla, as examples of holiness in the heart of the family, Cornelius, Saint Sebastian, and Saint Maurice among soldiers, and Constantine, Saint Helena, Saint Louis, and Saint Edward as examples among leaders. We even find instances of some who fell away in solitude, usually so helpful to perfection, and some who had reached the heights of spiritual life in the world, which seems so antagonistic to it. Be sure that wherever we may be, we can and must aim at the perfect life.

— Excerpt from *Introduction to the Devout Life,* Part 1: Chapter 3

V

Gentleness in Your Heart

The queen bee never takes wing without being surrounded by all her subjects; likewise, love never enters the heart without bringing all other virtues with it. Nevertheless, love does not set them all to work at once or equally, at all times and everywhere. The righteous man is "like a tree planted by the water side, that will bring forth his fruit in due season" (Ps 1:3). Likewise love, watering and refreshing the soul, causes it to bring forth good works, each in season as required. There is an old proverb that says the sweetest music is unwelcome at a time of mourning. Certain persons have made a great mistake when, seeking to cultivate some special virtue, they attempt to call everyone's attention to it on all occasions, worse yet if they take it upon themselves to censure those who do not make a continual study of this their favorite virtue.

Saint Paul tells us to "rejoice with those who rejoice, weep with those who weep" (Rm 12:15); and "Love is patient, kind, liberal, prudent, indulgent" (cf. 1 Cor 13:4ff.). At the same time, there are virtues of universal account, which must not only be called into action occasionally, but ought to spread their influence over everything. We do not very often come across opportunities for exercising strength, magnanimity, or munificence. However, gentleness, moderation, modesty, and humility are graces which ought to color everything we do. Though there may be virtues of a more exalted type, these virtues mentioned are the most continually called for in daily life. It is good, then, to have a ready stock in hand of these general virtues which we so frequently need to call upon.

— Excerpt from *Introduction to the Devout Life*, Part 3: Chapter 1

The holy oils, used by the Church according to apostolic tradition, are made of olive oil mixed with balm, which, among other things, represent two virtues especially noteworthy in our Lord, and which he has especially recommended to us, as though they, above all things, would draw us to him and teach us to imitate him: "Take my yoke upon you and learn from me, for I am meek and humble of heart" (Mt 11:29). Humility makes our lives pleasing to God, while meekness makes us acceptable to people. Balm, as I said before, sinking to the bottom of all liquids, is a figure of humility; and oil, floating as it does to the top, is a figure of gentleness and cheerfulness, rising above all things, and excelling in all things, the very flower of love, which, as Saint Bernard says, is perfected when it is not merely patient, but gentle and cheerful.

Be careful, then, that you keep this mystic chrism of gentleness and humility in your heart, for it is a strategy of the enemy to make people content with a superficial show of these graces, while they fail to examine their own inner hearts. So they fancy themselves to be gentle and humble while they are far from it. This is easily perceived, because, in spite of their ostentatious gentleness and humility, they are stirred up with pride and anger by the smallest wrong or contradiction. . . . True gentleness and humility will calm the burning which contradiction is apt to excite in our hearts. If, when stung by slander or someone's moodiness, we wax proud and swell with anger, it is a proof that our humility and gentleness are unreal, only an artificial show.

— Excerpt from *Introduction to the Devout Life,* Part 3: Chapter 8

VI

Never Give Way to Anger

When Joseph sent his brethren back from Egypt to his father's house, he only gave them one counsel, "Let there be no recriminations on the way" (Gn 45:24).

This earthly life is but the road to a blessed life. On the way let us not fall out with each other. Let us go on in the company of our brethren gently, peacefully, and kindly. I mean it when I say: if possible, never give way to anger, and under no pretext let anger and passion enter your heart. Saint James says, plainly and frankly, that "the wrath of a man does not accomplish the righteousness of God" (Jas 1:20). Without a doubt, it is a duty to oppose what is wrong and to steadily and firmly correct those for whom we are responsible, but we must also do so gently and quietly. . . . A correction given excitedly, however tempered by reason, never has so much effect as that which is given with calmness; for the reasonable soul is naturally subject to reason. Passion is mere tyranny, and in its throes, reason is ruled by it and becomes hateful, and what it claims to be a justice is really dishonor.

. . . Depend upon this, it is better to learn how to live without being angry than to imagine one can moderate and control anger lawfully. If through weakness and frailty one is overtaken by it, it is far better to put it away forcibly than to entertain it; for give anger even a little leeway, and it will become your master, like the serpent who easily insinuates its body wherever it has squeezed in its head. You ask how to put away anger: as soon as you feel the slightest resentment, collect yourself gently and seriously, not hastily or impetuously. Sometimes in a law court the officials who enforce quiet make more noise than those they want to hush; likewise, if you are impetuous in restraining your temper, you will throw your heart into worse confusion than before, and, amid the excitement, it will lose all self-control. . . . When we feel stirred with anger, we ought to call upon God for help, like the Apostles when they were tossed about with wind and storm, and he will surely say, "Peace, be still."

But even here I would again warn you, that your very prayers against the angry feelings which trouble you should be gentle, calm, and without vehemence. Remember this rule, whatever remedies against anger you may adopt. As soon as you are conscious of an angry act, atone for the fault by some speedy act of meekness toward the person who aroused your anger. It is a sovereign cure for untruthfulness to take back what you have falsely said as soon as you detect you are in falsehood; so, too, it is a good remedy for anger to make immediate amends by some opposite act of meekness. There is an old saying that fresh wounds quickly cared for are more swiftly healed.

Moreover, when there is nothing to stir your wrath, gather up a store of meekness and kindness, speaking and acting in things great and small as gently as possible. . . . So we must not only speak gently to our neighbor, but we must be filled, heart and soul, with gentleness; and we must not merely seek the sweetness of aromatic honey in courtesy and kindness with strangers, but also the sweetness of milk among those of our own family and our neighbors; a sweetness terribly lacking to some who are like angels on the street, but devils in their homes!

— Excerpt from *Introduction to the Devout Life,* Part 3: Chapter 8

VII

The Jewel of Poverty

If you are really poor, then do your best to be poor in spirit for love of God. Thus you will make a virtue out of necessity, and you will recognize the jewel of poverty for its true value. Its brilliance is not perceived in this world, but nevertheless it is very great. . . .

There are two great privileges connected with your poverty, through which you may acquire great merit. First, it is not your own choice which has made you poor. Now, whatever we accept as God's providential plan for us is pleasing in his sight, so long as we accept it heartily and out of love. A single-hearted acceptance of God's way purifies us greatly in any suffering.

The second privilege is that this poverty is real poverty. There is poverty which is so praised, caressed, petted, and cared for that it can hardly be called genuine. When poverty is despised, disdained, neglected, then it is real poverty. Now, most poverty in our world is this last kind, and those who are involuntarily poor are not thought much of. For that very reason their poverty is more truly poor than that of religious, even though religious poverty does have special and excellent grace, through the intention for which this vow was made.

Do not complain of your poverty. We only complain about what is unwelcome, and if poverty is unwelcome to you, then you are no longer poor in spirit. Do not be troubled about your need; in this need, through trust you will find the great grace of poverty. It would be overambitious to aim at being poor without suffering any inconvenience, because then you would be aiming for the credit of poverty while still wanting the convenience of riches.

— Excerpt from *Introduction to the Devout Life,* Part 3: Chapter 16

VIII

Virtues to Practice

Among those virtues which we are not obliged to practice by our own calling, we should choose to practice the most excellent, rather than the most pretentious. Comets look larger to us than the stars, but all the while comets are not nearly as important as the stars, and only seem so large to us because they are nearer to us than stars, and are made of a heavier material. So there are certain virtues which touch us very sensibly and are very tangible, so to speak; therefore, ordinary people give them the preference. Most people ordinarily value temporal almsgiving more than spiritual, and think more of fasting, exterior discipline, and bodily mortification than of meekness, cheerfulness, modesty, and other interior discipline; nevertheless, these are far better. Choose the best virtues, not the most highly esteemed; the most excellent, not the most visible; the truest, not the most conspicuous. It is a good thing for everybody to select some special virtue at which to aim, not to neglect the others, but to keep as an ideal.

Saint John, Bishop of Alexandria, saw a vision of a lovely maiden, brighter than the sun, in shining garments, and wearing a crown of olive leaves, who said to him, "I am the King's eldest daughter, and if you will accept me as your friend, I will bring you to see his face." John realized that it was compassion for the poor which God was commending to him, and from that time on he gave himself so heartily to practice it, that now he is universally known as Saint John the Almsgiver. Cassian relates how a certain devout maiden once asked Saint Athanasius to help her cultivate the virtue of patience, so he assigned her as a companion to a poor widow who was cross, irritable, and altogether intolerable, and whose perpetual fretfulness gave the pious lady abundant opportunities to practice forbearance and patience.

And so, some of God's servants devote themselves to nursing the sick, helping the poor, teaching little children the faith, seeking out the wanderers, building churches, adorning the altar, and making peace among all. In this, they resemble the embroiderers who work on all kinds of silks, stitching gold and silver onto them, and producing beautiful floral patterns. Those who undertake some special virtue use it as the ground of their personal spiritual "embroidery," and work all kinds of other graces onto it, setting their actions and affections in order by means of this, their chief "golden thread," which runs through them all.

— Excerpt from *Introduction to the Devout Life,* Part 3: Chapter 1

IX

True Zeal

Self-love often deceives us and leads us away, gratifying its own passions under the name of zeal. Zeal has once made use of anger, and now anger in its turn uses the name of zeal, in order to keep its shameful disorder covered under this. And mark that I say it makes use of the name of zeal; for it can make no use of zeal itself, since it is the property of all virtues, but especially of charity. . . .

A notorious sinner once went and threw himself at the feet of a good and worthy priest, protesting with much submission that he came to find a cure for his disease, that is, to receive the holy absolution of his faults. A certain monk called Demophilus, considering that, in his opinion, this poor penitent came too nigh the holy altar, fell into so violent a fit of anger, that throwing himself upon him, he kicked and pushed him thence with his feet, railing at the good priest, who according to his duty had mildly received this poor penitent. And then running up to the altar he took off the holy things which were there, and carried them away, lest, as he would have men think, the place should have been profaned by the sinner's approach. Now having finished this fair exploit of zeal, he stayed not yet there, but made a great rejoicing about the matter to the great Saint Denis the Areopagite in a letter, to which he received an excellent answer, worthy of the apostolic spirit wherewith that great disciple of Saint Paul was animated. For Saint Denis made Demophilus clearly see that his zeal had been at once indiscreet, imprudent, and impudent. For although the zeal for the honor due holy things was good and laudable, yet was it practiced against all reason, without any consideration or judgment, since he had employed kicks, outrages, railing, and reproaches, in a place, under circumstances, and against persons, whom and which he ought to have honored, loved, and respected. Thus his zeal could not be good, since it was practiced with such great disorder. In this same answer, that great saint recounts another admirable example of a great zeal, proceeding from a very good soul, which was, however,

spoilt and vitiated by the excess of ⸝
stirred up.

A pagan had led astray a Christi⸍
converted to the faith, causing hir⸍
Carpus, a man eminent for purity and saṇ⸍
as is very probable, was the bishop of Candia, conc⸍
against this pagan anger stronger than he had ever before
entertained. The bishop let himself be so far carried away
with this passion, that having risen at midnight to pray
according to his custom, he concluded that it was not reasonable that the wicked men should any longer be allowed
to live. With great indignation he beseeched the divine justice to strike down at once with his thunderbolts these two
sinners together, the pagan seducer and the Christian
seduced.

Hear, however, how God corrected the bitterness of
the passion which carried the poor Carpus beyond himself. First God made Carpus see, as had Saint Stephen,
the heavens open, and our Savior Jesus Christ seated
upon a great throne, surrounded with a multitude of
angels, who attended him in human form. Then he saw,
below, the earth gaping as a horrid and vast gulf, and the
two erring ones, to whom he had wished so much evil,
he saw upon the very brink of this precipice, trembling
and well-nigh paralyzed with fear, as being about to fall
into it. On the one side, these two were drawn by a

.de of serpents, which rising out of the gulf, ped themselves about their legs, and with their tails adually moved and provoked them to their fall; on the other side, certain men pushed and beat them to make them tumble in, so that they seemed on the point of being swallowed up in this abyss.

Now consider, my Theotimus,[3] the violence of the passion of Carpus: for, as he himself afterward recounted to Saint Denis, he never thought of contemplating our Savior and the angels, who showed themselves in the heavens, since he had been taking such pleasure in seeing the frightful distress of those two miserable wretches. His only frustration was that they were so slow in leaping to their peril and perishing, and so he had endeavored to help them himself by precipitating their fall. Seeing he could not push them over the edge at once, he was angry, and began to curse them, until at length, lifting up his eyes to heaven, he saw the sweet and most pitiful Savior. The Savior was moved by an extreme pity and compassion at what was happening, arose from his throne and descended to the place where the two miserable beings were, stretched out to them his helping hand, while the angels also, some on one side and some on another, caught hold of them to hinder them from falling into that dreadful gulf. At last the amiable and mild Jesus, turning himself to the wrathful Carpus, said, "No, Carpus, henceforth wreak your anger on me: for I am ready to suffer once more to save men and it would be a joy to me to do so, if it were possible to do so without sin on man's part. At any rate, think which would be the better for thee, to be in that gulf with the serpents, or to live with angels who are such great friends of men."

Theotimus, the holy man Carpus did have just reason to enter into zeal concerning these two men, and his zeal had rightly raised his anger against them. This anger once moved, however, left reason and zeal behind, transgressing all the terms and limits of holy love and consequently of zeal, which is but the fervor of charity. Anger had changed the hatred of sin into hatred of the sinner, and most sweet charity into an outrageous cruelty.

Thus there are persons who think one cannot be very zealous unless one is very angry, thinking that unless they spoil all, they can manage nothing. On the contrary, true zeal most rarely makes use of anger, for as we never apply the lancet to the sick save when it cannot possibly be helped, so holy zeal does not employ anger save in extreme necessities.

— Excerpt from *Treatise on the Love of God*, Part 10: Chapter 15

X

Do Small Things with Great Love

Great works do not lie always in our way, but every moment we may do little ones with excellence, that is, with a great love. Behold that saint, I beg you, who bestows a cup of cold water on the thirsty traveler. Such a one does what seems to be such a small thing when seen from the outside, but the intention, the sweetness, the love, with which he animates his work is so excellent, that it turns this simple water into water of life, and of eternal life.

The bees gather honey from the lily, the flag, the rose; yet they get as ample a booty from the little tiny rosemary flowers and thyme. Indeed, they draw not only more honey, but even better honey from these smaller flowers, for in these little vessels the honey, being more closely locked up, is kept better. Truly, in the low and little works of devotion, charity is not only practiced more frequently, but ordinarily more humbly too, and consequently more usefully and more holily.

That patience with the idiosyncrasies of another, that bearing with the clownish and troublesome actions and ways of our neighbor, those victories over our own moods and passions, those mortifications of our lesser inclinations, that effort against our aversions and repugnances, that heartfelt and sweet acknowledgment of our own imperfections, the continual pains we take to keep our souls in equanimity, that love of our littleness, that gentle and gracious welcome we give to the contempt and censure of our condition, of our life, of our conversation, of our actions. . . . Theotimus, all these things are more profitable to our souls than we can conceive, if heavenly love has the management of them.

— Excerpt from *Treatise on the Love of God,* Book 12: Chapter 6

XI

The Need for Patience

What I have noticed with doves is that they mourn in the same way that they rejoice, and that they sing always the same note, both in their songs of joy as in the songs in which they lament and express their complaints and sorrow. Whether they be joyous or sad, they never change their tune. Their cooing is ever the same.

It is this holy evenness of spirit which we ought to have. I do not say evenness of humor or of inclination, but of spirit, for we ought to make no account of the fretting of the inferior part of the soul. It is the inferior part of the soul which causes disquietude and caprice when the superior part doesn't do its duty by rendering itself supreme, and doesn't keep a vigilant watch to discern its enemies and be aware of the tumults and assaults raised against it by the inferior part. These tumults spring from our senses and our inclinations and passions to make war upon the reason and to subject reason to their laws. I say, moreover, that we ought always to keep ourselves firm and resolute in the superior part of our soul, to follow virtue and to keep ourselves in a continual evenness amidst events favorable or adverse, in desolation as in consolation.

Holy Job provided us with an example on this subject, for he never sang except in the same key. When God multiplied his property, gave him children, and sent to him at his will everything which he could desire in this life, what did Job say except, blessed be the name of the Lord? It was his canticle of love, which he sang on every occasion. For behold Job reduced to the extremity of affliction. What does he do? He sings his song of lamentation in the same notes which he chanted in his season of joy. "If we have received good things," said he, "at the hand of God, why should we not receive evil? The Lord gave, and the Lord has taken away. Blessed be the name of the Lord." No other canticle, be the time what it may, but this, "Blessed be the name of the Lord."

Oh, how similar was that holy soul to the dove, which rejoices and laments always in the same note! Thus may we do; and on every occasion thus may we receive goods, evils, consolations, afflictions, from the hand of the Lord, ever singing that same sweetest canticle, "Blessed be the holy name of God," and always in continual evenness.

Never let us act like those who weep when consolation fails them, and only sing when it has returned, resembling apes and baboons which are sad and furious when the weather is gloomy and rainy, and never cease leaping and playing when the weather is fair and serene.

— Excerpt from *Practical Piety*, Part 3: Chapter 30

I remember that you said to me how burdensome you felt the multiplicity of your affairs, and I replied to you that it was an excellent means for the acquisition of true and solid virtue. The multiplicity of affairs is a continual martyrdom. For as the flies weary and annoy those who travel in summer more than the fatigue of the journey itself, so the diversity and multiplicity of affairs give more trouble than the weight of the affairs themselves.

You have need of patience. I hope that God will give it to you if you diligently ask it of him and force yourself to practice it faithfully by preparing yourself for it every morning, by a special application of some point in your meditation, and resolving to settle yourself in patience throughout the course of the day or as often as you feel yourself distracted with business.

Lose no occasion, however trifling, of exercising sweetness of heart toward anyone. Do not reckon on being able to succeed in your affairs by your own industry, but only by the assistance of God. Consequently repose yourself in his bosom, knowing that he will do what is best for you, provided that you use a sweet diligence on your part.

I say a sweet diligence, because there is a kind of violent diligence which perils the heart and the business you transact. Such diligence does not deserve the name, but should rather be called anxiety and trouble. My God! We shall soon be in eternity, and then we shall see what a little matter are all the affairs of the world, and of how small consequence it was whether they were done or not done. Nevertheless, we make ourselves anxious regarding them as though they were great things.

Attend diligently to your affairs, but know that you have no affairs of greater importance than those of your salvation, and the paving of the way to a true and solid devotion. Have patience with all, but principally with yourself. I mean, do not make yourself unhappy about your imperfections, but always have the courage to rise above them. I am very glad that you make a fresh beginning every day. There is no better means for achieving the spiritual life than always to recommence, and never to suppose that you have done enough.

— Excerpt from *Practical Piety*, Part 3: Chapter 49

XII

Do Not Lose Your Inner Peace

I have heard of all your troubles and I have commended them to our Lord, asking him to bless them with that sacred benediction which he gives his chosen servants, so that they may all turn to the sanctification of his holy name and of your soul.

I must confess that to my mind, of all afflictions and evils, lawsuits excite my pity most, because they are so dangerous to the soul. How many people I have seen bearing the sting of sickness or the loss of friends patiently, who yet have lost their inward peace under the harassment of legal affairs or lawsuits! The reason, or more correctly the cause is this: we are not ready to believe that God makes use of such a trial to prove us, because it seems to come direct from the hand of man. While we dare not kick against an all-wise, all-good Providence, we do kick against the fellow creatures who trouble us, and grow enraged with them, not without great risk of a loss of charity, the only loss we need really fear in this life. Well now, my dear daughter, when can we better testify our faithfulness to our Savior, than on such occasions? What time is more fitting for bridling heart, judgment, and tongue, than when we are toiling along such crooked paths and going so near the edge of a precipice? For God's sake, my dear daughter, do not let slip a time so eminently calculated for spiritual progress without laying in a fresh store of patience, humility, gentleness, and love of abjection. Remember that our Lord never spoke one word against those that condemned him. He did not judge them. Instead, even though he was unjustly condemned, he was gentle as a lamb and his only revenge was prayer for his enemies. We, on the other hand, judge everyone, our antagonists and our judges. We bristle with complaints and reproaches. Believe me, dear daughter, we must be steadfast in loving our neighbor. I say this with my whole heart, without any consideration as to your individual opponents or anything concerning the matter, caring for nothing save your perfection. Here, however, I must stop, nor did I mean to say so much. You have God always with you, if you will. Does not that make you rich enough? May his will be your rest, his cross your glory.

— Excerpt from a letter to a lady involved in legal affairs, September 19, 1610

XIII

Avoid Vanity and Ambition

So at last your sails are spread and you are about to enter the high seas of the world and the court. May God vouchsafe to guide and keep you in his holy hand!

I am not so timid as some people, nor do I hold this manner of life to be the most dangerous for well-trained souls who are bold and brave. There are but two great perils to dread: vanity, which is the ruin of sensual, indolent, self-indulgent, effeminate characters; and ambition, which destroys presumptuous, audacious minds. Vanity implies a lack of courage: the vain man has not strength to seek after real, well-earned approbation, and so he is satisfied with what is unreal and hollow. Ambition, instead, is courage carried to excess, which goes headlong in pursuit of glory and honor, regardless of all reason and rule. So vanity leads a man into the frivolities which are acceptable to foolish women and other weak persons, but which are despicable in the eyes of nobler spirits; and ambition makes him grasp at honors which he has not earned. It makes him put too high a price upon himself and upon the merits of his forefathers on which he strives to build his fabric.

Now, dear sir, as you wish for my advice, I would say this: strengthen your mind against all this, by spiritual and sacred food, which will enable you to resist both vanity and ambition. Be steadfast in frequent Communion. Believe me, nothing will so tend to confirm you in the right way. Place yourself under the guidance of some good confessor and ask him to call you to account for any neglect you may ever fall into in this matter. Let your confessions be humble and made with a real and express purpose of amendment.

I entreat you never to omit asking upon your knees for the help of our Lord before you go forth in the morning and in like manner ask forgiveness of all your faults before going to bed at night.

Especially avoid bad books. Let nothing induce you to be led away by the writings which captivate certain weak minds by their vain subtleties; such works I mean as those of Rabelais [4] and others, who affect to throw doubt and contempt on everything and scoff at all our venerable doctrines and precepts. Keep books of a solid character, especially Christian and spiritual works, at hand and refresh yourself with them from time to time.

I would have you cultivate a gentle, sincere courtesy, which offends no one, but wins everybody. Be more ready to seek love than honor. Never jest at the expense of another, never be sarcastic, never affront another or be affronted.

Take care not to get involved in flirtations and do not allow your affections to carry you away against judgment and reason. Once you let emotions get the lead and they are apt to make a sorry slave of the judgment and lead to results you are sure to repent of.

In manner, appearance, conversation, and all such things, I would have you make an open profession that you propose to live virtuously, wisely, and steadfastly, as a Christian should. Virtuously, so that no one may attempt to lead you into any debauchery; wisely, without any exaggerated outward demonstrations; steadily, because unless you show that you have a steadfast will and even mind, evil men will seek to tempt and delude you; as a Christian should, because some men profess a philosophic virtue, which is but a mere phantom at best. We who know that we can have no possible goodness save through the grace of our Lord, are bound to live by the rules of piety and religion, or else all our virtue will prove a shadow and an empty imagination.

It is most important that you should let it be known from the first what you mean to be. There should be no doubt about the matter. Also it will help you tremendously if you have some like-minded friends with whom you can exchange counsel and sympathy. Unquestionably, the friendships we have with right-minded people tend not a little to keep us straight.

There is one special point on which you must permit me to touch. I dread, sir, lest you should again take to gaming. It would be an exceeding evil, and in a few days would lead to complete dissipation, withering the bloom of your good desires. It is but an idle pursuit, at best. At worst, we could dwell upon the angry passions, the dishonesty and despair, from which few gamblers are exempted. I would wish for you a vigorous heart and a disposition to avoid bodily ease, whether in food, sleep, or anything else. A really noble mind despises mere luxury and self-indulgence. But I touch upon this point because our Lord says, "They who wear soft clothing are in kings' houses;" not as meaning that all dwelling there must be luxurious, but that many found in such quarters are so disposed. Of course I am not alluding to the exterior, but to the interior life. In short, I would have you keep the body in hand and make it sometimes forego pleasant things and endure hardness and abstinence, so that the higher nature may assert and maintain its superiority over that which is lower.

Be a very earnest Christian, that is, devout, pious, spiritually minded; as Saint Paul says, "He that is spiritual judges all things" (1 Cor 2:15), that is, he knows the right time and place for the practice of every virtue.

Often call to mind the thought that in this world we hang between heaven and hell and that our last step will land us in one or the other. Remember, too, that we do not know when we shall make that last step and that he who would make it well must strive to make every step in the fear of God.

O blessed, endless eternity! And blessed are they that rightly ponder it! All that we do here for a brief uncertain time is but child's play. It would be less than worthless, save that it is the passage to eternity. But for that reason we must give good heed to our time and its use here, in order through a right use thereof to win our lasting good.

Think of me, I pray you, as wholly yours, as in truth I am in our Lord, wishing you all happiness in this world, but still more in the next. May God bless you and have you in his holy keeping.

To end as I began—you are taking to the high seas of life, but do not change your captain, your sails, your anchor, or your breeze. Ever keep Jesus for your captain, his cross for your mast, whereon to spread the sails of good resolutions; let your anchor be a deep unfailing trust in him and then go daily on. May the propitious breeze of heavenly grace fill your sails more and more and carry you safely and happily into the haven of a blessed eternity.

— Excerpt from a letter to a gentleman beginning
a career at court, December 8, 1610

XIV

Do Not Be Overwhelmed

I entreat you, my dear daughter, keep close to Jesus Christ and our Lady and your good angel, in all your business, so that the multiplicity of affairs may not overwhelm you, or their difficulty trouble you.

Attend to them one by one, as best you can. To do this, give your mind steadily to your work, though quietly and gently. If God vouchsafes you success, we will bless him; if he does not do so, we will equally bless him. It is enough that you sincerely do your very best. Neither our Lord nor common sense will call us to account for results or events. We are only responsible for steady, honest diligence in our work. This alone depends upon ourselves, success does not.

God will bless your good intentions in this journey and in your undertaking to order matters well and wisely for your son. He will reward you either by a successful end to your labor, or by a holy humility and resignation under disappointment.

— Excerpt from a letter to Madame de Chantal when absent on family business, September 10, 1611

———— ୴୶ ————

Do not be disheartened: God will never lose sight of you or your flock, so long as you trust in him. Do not let yourself be disgusted, my dear daughter, or allow contradictions to weaken your mind.

Whenever was God's service free from contradictions, especially in the beginning of good works? I must, however, tell you honestly that what I fear most in all this is a temptation to set up dislike and aversion between you and N _____. It is a common temptation where two people are brought thus into collision; it is a temptation incidental to the most angelic minds on earth, as we see by its arising even among the greatest saints. Our folly, as children of Adam, will be the ruin of us all, unless we are saved from it through charity.

When I see two apostles like Saints Paul and Barnabas separating because they cannot agree concerning a third companion, I look indulgently upon these little dislikes, so long as they do not hinder the work, even as the apostles parting asunder did not hinder their mission. If some such thing happens between you two women, it is no great marvel, always supposing that it does not last. But, all the same, my dear daughter, brace your mind anew and be sure that what you do is of great consequence. Bear patiently, do not be pettish, soften all asperities. Remember that this lady is intending to serve God according to her light, as you are according to yours. Recollect that you ought both to bear with and help one another for the love of Christ. Two or three years will soon pass by, but eternity remains.

Your bodily ailments make the matter worse. However, you will be strengthened if you call to mind the help promised to those who suffer. Finally, be on your guard against discouragement. Believe me, we must sow in labor, in perplexity, in anguish, if we would reap in joy, in consolation, in happiness. Holy confidence in God softens everything, penetrates everything, establishes everything. I am assuredly yours wholly, my dear daughter, and I do not cease to pray that God will make you holy, strong, steadfast, and perfect in his service. I salute our dear sisters cordially and entreat them to pray for my soul, which is for ever bound up with yours and theirs in the joy of our Lord and Savior, Jesus.

— Excerpt from an undated letter to Madame de Chantal

XV

Attached to the Will of God

Keep, I pray you, your heart exalted very high; attach it indissolubly to the will of that most merciful and fatherly heart of our God. Let it forever be obeyed, and supremely obeyed, by our souls. So long as God wills that we are to be in the world for the love of himself, remain there willing and cheerfully.

Many leave the world, who, for all that, do not leave themselves; but seek instead their own taste, their ease, their contentment; and these persons are marvelously eager for this; for the self-love which urges them on is a turbulent, impetuous, and unruly love.

Let us not be of this class; let us leave the world to serve God, to follow God, to love God; and in this frame of mind, so long as God wills that we serve, follow, and love him in the world, we will remain there with a good heart; for since it is only that holy service which we desire, in whatever place we perform it, we shall be contented.

Abide in peace; do that well on account of which you remain in the world; do it with a good heart and be assured that God will esteem it of more worth at your hands, than if you left the world a hundred times to please your own will and inclination.

As to your other desire, it is a good one; but, O my God, it is not worth setting your heart upon. Let us recommend it to God; let us do sweetly whatever can be done to attain success in it, as I shall do for my part. And if the eye of God, which penetrates the future, seeing perchance that this would not turn out either to his glory, or as we intend it, we must not lose one hour's sleep for the sake of it.

The world will talk: What will people say? All this is nothing to those who look not upon time except in the light of eternity.

I will endeavor to keep the affair in progress, so that we may be able to see it completed; for you do not desire it more than I do. But if it is not pleasing to God, it is not pleasing either to me or to you. Abide in peace, with a singular love of the divine will and providence. Abide with our Savior crucified planted in the midst of your heart.

I saw, awhile ago, a girl who was carrying a pail of water on her head, in the midst of which she had placed a piece of wood. I wished to know why she did this; and she told me that it was to stop the motion of the water, for fear it might be spilt. So henceforth, I said, we must place the cross in the midst of our hearts, to stop the movements of our affections in that wood and by that wood, so that they may not be spilt out in disquietudes and in troubles of spirit.

— Excerpt from *Practical Piety*, Part 1: Chapter 3

XVI

Cast Yourself on God

You ask me whether a soul, having the consciousness of her misery, can go to God with great confidence.

Now, I reply, that not only the soul which has the consciousness of her misery can have a great confidence in God, but that she cannot have a true confidence unless she has the knowledge of this misery, for this knowledge, and this admission of our misery, introduces us to God.

Therefore all the great saints, such as Job, David, and the others, began all their prayers with the confession of their misery; so that it is a good thing to be conscious that one is poor, vile, abject, unworthy to appear before God.

That proverb so famous among the ancients, *know thyself,* at the same time that it applies to the greatness and excellence of the soul—that we should not abuse and profane it by things unworthy of its nobility—also applies to the knowledge of our own unworthiness, imperfection, and misery, so that the more we feel ourselves to be miserable, the more we should trust in the goodness and mercy of God. Indeed between God's mercy and our misery there is a bond so close, that the one cannot exercise itself without the other. If God had not created man, he still would have been truly all good, but he would not have been actually merciful, mercy is only exercised toward the miserable.

You see, then, that the more we feel ourselves miserable, the more we have occasion to put our trust in God, since we have nothing to rest upon, to enable us to put our trust in ourselves.

Mistrust in ourselves arises from the knowledge of our imperfections. It is good to mistrust ourselves; but to what advantage would it be for us to do that, were it not to throw all our confidence in God and to wait on his mercy? The faults and unfaithfulness which we daily commit ought to bring much confusion upon us when we would approach our Lord. Thus, we read that great souls, like Saint Catherine of Siena and Saint Teresa, had these great confusions when they had fallen into some fault; and it is very reasonable that, having offended God, we should retire awhile in humility and remain confused. The same thing often happens to us when we have offended a friend; we are ashamed to approach him. But we must not stop there; for it would be no great thing, this annihilation and divesting one of self, which is done by acts of confusion, if it was not in order to throw ourselves wholly on God by confidence.

And if you feel no such confidence, cease not, on that account, from making these acts and from saying to our Lord, just the same: "O Lord, though I have no feeling of confidence in thee, I nevertheless know I have no hope but in thy goodness; so I abandon myself wholly into thy hands."

It is always in our power to make these acts and although we have difficulty in them, still there is no impossibility. It is precisely on these occasions and in the midst of these difficulties, that we ought to testify faithfulness to our Lord. For even though we do these acts without sensible pleasure and without any satisfaction, we must not on that account be discouraged, for our Lord loves them better so. Furthermore, do not tell me that you say this prayer, indeed, but it is only with your lips, for if the heart willed it not, the lips would not say a word. Having done so, remain in peace and without attending to your disquietude, speak to our Lord of something else.

It is, then very good to suffer confusion when we have the knowledge and the feeling of our own misery; but we must not stop there, nor fall, for that reason, into discouragement. Instead, we must lift up our hearts to God with a holy confidence, the foundation of which must be in him and in ourselves, inasmuch as we change and he never changes, but remains always as good and as merciful when we are feeble and imperfect, as when we are strong and perfect.

I am accustomed to say that the throne of God's mercy is our misery. In proportion, therefore, to the greatness of our misery ought to be the greatness of our confidence.

— Excerpt from *Practical Piety*, Part 1: Chapters 4 and 5.

XVII

Unite Perfectly
to Divine Goodness

It is necessary you should know, that to abandon one's soul and to allow one's self, as it were, to drop out of one's own hands into God's, means nothing else but parting with our own will to give it unto God; for it would be to little purpose our renouncing and surrendering ourselves, if this were not done in order to unite ourselves perfectly to the divine goodness. To do otherwise would be to resemble those philosophers who in an extraordinary manner abandoned themselves and all things for the sake of vain pretensions and to devote themselves to philosophy. Epictetus was an instance of this. He was a slave and his master wished to free him because of his great wisdom. However, Epictetus did not choose to gain his liberty since it would have been at the cost of renouncing his lofty contemplations. He, therefore, remained a slave for the rest of his life, and in such poverty, that, after his death, the only property found about him was a lamp, which was sold at a very high price, because it had belonged to so great a man.

As for us, we should not desire to abandon ourselves except to put ourselves at the mercy of God's will. There are many who say to our Lord, "I give myself unto thee without any reserve," but there are very few who embrace the practice of this abandonment, which is nothing other than a perfect resignation to receive all sorts of events according as they occur by order of the providence of God: affliction as well as consolation, sickness as well as health, poverty as well as riches, contempt as well as honor, disgrace as well as glory.

I mean this in reference to the superior part of our soul; for there is no doubt that the inferior parts and our natural inclinations always tend instead in the direction of honor than of contempt, of riches than of poverty, although everyone knows that contempt and poverty are more agreeable to God than honor and abundance.

Now, in order to achieve this abandonment, one must obey the expressed will of God and that of his good pleasure. The expressed will of God includes his commandments, his counsels, his inspirations and the rules and ordinances of our superiors.

The will of his good pleasure regards the issues of things which we cannot foresee; for example, I know not if I am to die tomorrow. I perceive that it is the good pleasure of God that I die and consequently I abandon myself to his good pleasure and die with a good heart. In like manner, I know not whether in the coming year all the fruits of the earth will not be spoilt by storms and tempests; if it happens that they are so, or that a pestilence befalls us, or any similar events, it is evident that such is the good pleasure of God and consequently I conform myself to it.

It may occur that you have no consolation in your religious exercises; it is certain that such is the good pleasure of God, to which therefore we must conform ourselves; and the same for all things that happen, excepting, however, sin and the loss of one's soul, to which we are never permitted to consent under the notion of conforming ourselves to God's will, which would be one of the grossest of delusions.

We must, moreover, observe that there are things in which it is necessary to join the expressed will of God to that of his good pleasure. For example, if I fall sick of a violent fever, I perceive in that event that the good pleasure of God is that I remain in a state of indifference to health or sickness. However, the expressed will of God is that if I am not under obedience I should call in the physician and apply all the remedies I can (I do not say those of the most costly kind, but such as are common and ordinary), and that those who are under obedience should receive the remedies and treatment afforded them with simplicity and obedience. This God has declared to us by imparting to remedies their efficacy: the sacred Scriptures teach us this and the Church orders it.

After taking these measures, a soul perfectly abandoned to God remains so indifferent whether the sickness prevails over the remedy or the remedy prevails over the sickness, that if sickness and health were placed before her and if our Lord said to her, "If you choose health, I will not for that reason take from you one grain of my grace; if you choose sickness, in like manner, I will not enrich you with one grain additional; but in the choice of sickness there is somewhat more of my good pleasure," the soul which is entirely abandoned into the hands of our Lord will without hesitation choose sickness, solely because there is in it more of the good pleasure of God. Yes, even were it to follow that she should remain on a sick bed all her life, without doing anything else but suffer, she would not, for all the world could give, desire any other state than that. Thus the saints who are in heaven have such a union with the will of God, that if there were somewhat more of his good pleasure in hell, they would quit paradise to go there.

— Excerpt from *Practical Piety*, Part 1: Chapter 7

XVIII

Soften Your Sorrows

You ask me how I wish that you should act on an interview with the gentleman who killed your husband. I reply, that it is not necessary you should seek either day or occasion for it; but if such an occasion does present itself, I wish you to keep your heart calm, gracious, and compassionate.

I know that, doubtless, your heart will be stirred and agitated, that your blood will boil; but what matters that? Our dear Savior felt this at the sight of dead Lazarus and of the representation of his passion. Yes, but what does the Scripture say? That on both occasions he lifted up his eyes to heaven. God makes us see in these emotions that we are made of flesh and blood as well as spirit.

I have explained myself sufficiently. I reply, I do not wish that you should seek an interview with this poor man, but that you should be condescending to those who wished you should grant one; and that you should show yourself resigned to all things, even the death of your husband, or that of your father, of your children, and of your nearest relations; yes, even your own death in the death and in the love of our sweet Savior. Courage! Let us go forward and let us practice these lowly and common, yet solid, holy, and excellent virtues. Abide in peace; and keep yourself on your feet and on the side of heaven. God has held you with his goodness in your affliction. He will assuredly always do so. "My God," said Saint Gregory to an afflicted bishop, "how can it be that our hearts, which are already in heaven, are agitated by the accidents of the earth?" It was well said. The mere sight of our dear crucified Jesus can soften in a moment all our sorrows, which are only flowers in comparison with those thorns. Then our great meeting-point is in that eternity, the reward of which we have in view. How can anything affect us which is terminated by time.

Continue to unite yourself more and more with this Savior. Plunge your heart into that abyss of charity which is his, and let us say always, with all our heart, "Let me die and let Jesus live." Our death will be happy if it be in his life. *I live,* said the Apostle; but he corrects himself immediately, *now not I, but Christ lives in me* (Gal 2: 20).

May you be blessed, with the benediction which the divine goodness has prepared for hearts which love. And courage! God is good to us: let all else be evil to us, what matters it? Live joyously before him. Years go on and eternity approaches: may we so employ those years in the divine love that we may enjoy an eternity in his glory!

— Excerpt from *Practical Piety,* Part 2: Chapter 28

XIX

Be Content

What is humility? Is it the knowledge of our misery and poverty? Yes, says Saint Bernard; but that is human humility. What, then, is Christian humility? It is the love of this poverty and lowliness, in consideration of that of our Lord.

Know that you are a creature, poor and little. Love to be such; glory in being nothing. Be well content in your place since your misery becomes the object of God's goodness and on you he exercises his great mercy.

Among the poor, those who are the most miserable and most pitiable believe that they are most likely to attract the compassion of those who give alms. We ourselves are nothing more than poor people. The most miserable among us is in the best condition to attract the mercy of God who looks most willingly on the most pitiable of his creatures.

Let us humble ourselves, I beseech you, and let us preach nothing but our wounds at the gate of the temple of divine goodness. Remember, however, to preach them joyfully, consoling yourself at being altogether empty, that God may satisfy you with his kingdom. Be sweet and affable to everyone, except to those who would rob you of your glory, which is your misery. *I glory in my infirmities*, says the apostle (2 Cor 12: 9). *And to me to die is gain* (Phil 1:21) rather than to lose my glory. Do you see he preferred rather to die than to lose his infirmities, which are his glory?

You must take good care of your misery, your lowliness, for God takes care of it, as he did of that of the Holy Virgin (cf. Lk 1: 48). *Man sees those things that appear, but the LORD sees the heart* (1 Sam 16: 7). If he sees the lowliness in our hearts, he will give us great graces.

This humility preserves chastity. This is why in the Canticles that beautiful soul is called the *lily of the valley* (Sg 2:1). Keep yourself, therefore, cheerfully humble before God, but keep yourself equally cheerful and humble before the world. Be very content if the world makes no account of you. If it values you, cheerfully ridicule it and laugh at its judgment and at your misery which it accepts. If it does not value you, comfort yourself cheerfully on the ground that at least in this instance the world follows the truth.

As to your exterior, do not affect visible humility, but also do not avoid it. Embrace it, but always cheerfully. I approve of your sometimes humbling yourself to lowly services, even for inferiors and proud persons, for the sick and poor, for those about you in the house and out of it. However, always do this with simplicity and cheerfulness. Offices of a humble kind that belong to exterior humility are only the shell. Nevertheless, it is the shell that preserves the fruit.

To understand what is meant by the spirit of humility, it is necessary to know that just as there is a difference between pride, the habit of pride, and the spirit of pride, there is also a difference between humility, the habit of humility, and the spirit of humility.

If you carry out an act of pride, there is pride. If you carry out such acts on every occasion and wherever you go, there is the habit of pride. If you take pleasure in those acts and are on the look-out for them, there is the spirit of pride.

In the same way, if you do an act of humility, there is humility. If you do acts of humility on all occasions and wherever you go, there is the habit of humility. If you take pleasure in humiliation and are on the look-out for abjection in everything, there is the spirit of humility.

To have the spirit of humility, therefore, it is not sufficient to do some acts of humility, nor even to do such acts often. Instead, it is necessary in all that we do, say, or desire, that our principal end should be to humble and abase ourselves and that we should take pleasure in humiliation and seek for abjection in all things.

It is a good practice of humility never to look upon the actions of our neighbors, except to remark the virtues that are in them, but never their imperfections, for so long as we are not in charge of others, we must never turn our eyes and still less our attention to their imperfections.

We must always put the best judgment that we can upon what we see our neighbor do. In doubtful matters, we ought to persuade ourselves that what we noticed is not bad, but that it is our own imperfections that cause such a thought to arise in our minds. . . . In cases in which we see another do something clearly wrong, we ought to have compassion for our neighbor and humble ourselves for these defects as if they were our own, begging God for the other's amendment with the same heart we would for our own were we subject to the same defects.

But what can we do, you say, to acquire this spirit of humility?

Oh, there is no other way but frequent repetition of its acts. Humility makes us annihilate ourselves in all those things which are not necessary for our advancement in grace, such as good speaking, noble manners, great talents for the management of affairs, and a great spirit of eloquence and the like. In these exterior things we ought to desire that others should succeed better than ourselves.

— Excerpt from *Practical Piety*, Part 3: Chapters 9 and 10

XX

Live in the Spirit

Since my return from the visit, I felt some symptoms of fever. Our physician would not order me any remedy except rest and I obeyed him. You know also that the remedy I willingly order is tranquillity and that I always forbid excitement. This is why, in this bodily repose, I have thought of the spiritual repose which our hearts ought to feel in the will of God, whatever portion it assigns to us. Let us live as long as it pleases God in this vale of miseries, with an entire submission to his holy and sovereign will. I thought the other day of what writers say concerning the halcyons, little birds which float on the waves of the sea. It is that they make nests so round and compact that the water of the sea cannot penetrate them. At the top of the nest there is a small hole. It is only through this hole that they can breathe. In these nests they lodge their young, so that if the sea surprises them, they may swim safely, the nests floating on the waves without filling or sinking. The air which comes through the hole serves as counterpoise and so balances these little balls or boats so that they never overturn. Oh, how I wish that our hearts were as compact and as well sealed on all sides, so that if the troubles and tempests of the world seized them, they might never penetrate them. How I desire that there were no opening but on the side of heaven, to breathe unto our Savior! While the halcyons build their nests and their young are still too tender to bear the dashing of the waves, God has care for them and pities them, keeping the sea from seizing the nests and carrying them away. O God! In the same way this sovereign goodness will secure the nest of our hearts for his holy love against all the assaults of the world, where he will defend us from being assailed. Oh, how I love those birds which are surrounded with water, living only on the air and seeing only the sky! They swim like the fishes and sing like birds. What pleases me more is that their anchor is thrown on high, and not beneath, to steady them against the waves. May sweet Jesus make us such, that, surrounded with the world and the flesh, we may live in the spirit; that, among the vanities of the earth, we may always look to heaven; that, living among men, we may always praise him with the angels; and that the security of our hopes may always be on high and in paradise. Everywhere and in everything, may holy love be our great love.

— Excerpt from *Practical Piety*, Part 3: Chapter 17

Notes

1. A provost is someone put in charge to represent an authority, as the provost of a university or a cathedral. Since the bishop's official seat was in Annecy, Francis was appointed his representative in Geneva. In order to discharge this duty, he needed to be ordained a priest.

2. These two books of spiritual direction were addressed to representative laypersons. *Introduction to the Devout Life* (1609) to a woman: Philothea; *Treatise on the Love of God* (1616) to a man: Theotimus. Both names mean "lover of God."

3. See previous note.

4. Francois Rabelais (1494–1553) was a Renaissance humanist, writer, and doctor whose books often ridiculed the religious practice and moral teaching of the Church.

Bibliography

De Sales, Francis. *Practical Piety Set Forth by Saint Francis de Sales, Bishop and Prince of Geneva, Collected From His Letters and Discourses, and Now First Translated into English.* London: Burns and Lambert, 1851.

_____. *A Selection from the Spiritual Letters of Saint Francis de Sales.* Translated by H. L. Sidney Lear. London: Rivingtons, 1871.

_____. *Letters to Persons in Religion.* Translated and edited by Rev. H. B. Mackey, OSB. London: Burns, Oates & Washbourne, 1908.

_____. *Introduction to the Devout Life,* A new translation. Edited by Rev. W. J. B. Richards. London: Burns, 1878.

_____. *Treatise on the Love of God.* Translated by Rev. H. B. Mackey, OSB. London: Burns & Oates, 1884.

Henry-Coüannier, Maurice. *Saint Francis De Sales and His Friends.* Translated by Veronica Morrow. Staten Island, NY: Alba House, 1973.

For books by and about Saint Francis de Sales go to www.desalesresource.org.

For a bibliography of the English language works about and by Saint Francis de Sales go to the website prepared by Joseph Boenzi, SDB: http://www4.desales.edu/~salesian/resources/bibliographies/fdsbibli.html

Pauline
BOOKS & MEDIA

The Daughters of St. Paul operate book and media centers at the following addresses. Visit, call, or write the one nearest you today, or find us on the World Wide Web, www.pauline.org.

CALIFORNIA
3908 Sepulveda Blvd, Culver City, CA 90230	310-397-8676
935 Brewster Avenue, Redwood City, CA 94063	650-369-4230
5945 Balboa Avenue, San Diego, CA 92111	858-565-9181

FLORIDA
145 S.W. 107th Avenue, Miami, FL 33174	305-559-6715

HAWAII
1143 Bishop Street, Honolulu, HI 96813	808-521-2731
Neighbor Islands call:	866-521-2731

ILLINOIS
172 North Michigan Avenue, Chicago, IL 60601	312-346-4228

LOUISIANA
4403 Veterans Memorial Blvd, Metairie, LA 70006	504-887-7631

MASSACHUSETTS
885 Providence Hwy, Dedham, MA 02026	781-326-5385

MISSOURI
9804 Watson Road, St. Louis, MO 63126	314-965-3512

NEW YORK
64 W. 38th Street, New York, NY 10018	212-754-1110

PENNSYLVANIA
Philadelphia—relocating	215-676-9494

SOUTH CAROLINA
243 King Street, Charleston, SC 29401	843-577-0175

VIRGINIA
1025 King Street, Alexandria, VA 22314	703-549-3806

CANADA
3022 Dufferin Street, Toronto, ON M6B 3T5	416-781-9131

¡También somos su fuente para libros,
videos y música en español!